W9-ADF-895

the
ART OF LOVE

the

ART OF LOVE

new & selected poems

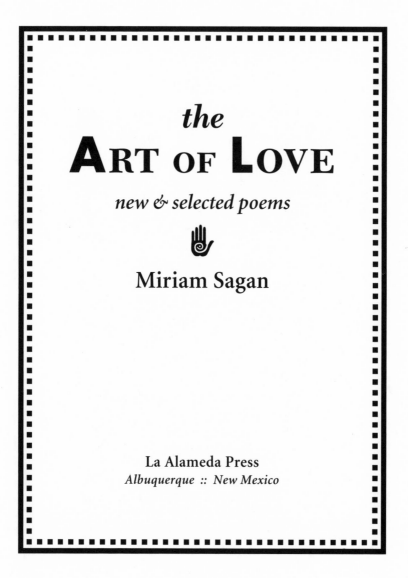

Miriam Sagan

La Alameda Press
Albuquerque :: New Mexico

Acknowledgments

"Invocation," "A Headless Venus," "Beneath the Tracks,"
"Judith and Holophernes," "Marriage," and "The Sailor"
first appeared in a chapbook, *THE DARK FACES OF LOVE,*
(with Joan Logghe) from Yoo-Hoo Press, 1992.
"The Lonesome Death of Federico García Lorca" appeared in ASYLUM,
"Shell in the Desert" and "Skunk Cabbage" in NOCTILUCA,
"The Matisse Network" in FREE LUNCH,
"Bette Davis: In Out of the Rain" in BLUE MESA REVIEW,
"Pocahontas Electric" in APOSTROPHE (England),
"Peak Completely Obscured by Cloud" in FISH DRUM.

·

The eight poems of the MARGARET SANGER cycle
were written with a grant from *Money For Women~*
The Barbara Deming Foundation.
Many thanks for the support are due to them.

AND thanks to Robert Winson, for inspiration Above & Beyond.

ISBN 0-9631909-2-x

La Alameda Press
9636 Guadalupe Trail NW
Albuquerque, New Mexico 87114

Contents

■ ■ ■ ■ ■ ■ ■

THE ART OF LOVE

1. Invocation

New moon, darkness, a white
Chrysanthemum
In an antique silver vase
Not belonging to your grandmother
But gift of a sometime lover.
Miriam, you say, why don't you
Tell the truth for once
All those stories about love
You save up like spare change
In a jam jar
Men and women, women and women, men with men
Everything you've ever done
Or heard about
Or wanted to do again
And please, you say, don't start
Learning ancient Greek
In preparation
Or translating awkwardly from the Latin
You know it all—
Bad-boy Cupid on his motorcycle,
Weapons and border skirmishes,
A hard bed,
Someone asking for money,

An abortion, and
The throb of Isis Isis Isis
Just before the room shifts red.
There is no remedy for love
Even the poet who should know
Simply said: Love is a kind of war
And no assignment for cowards.

THE ART OF LOVE

2. A Headless Venus

Up on the tar roof,
City in cicada dark
She's wrapped in a sheet
Woman who will break my heart
Fair-haired, her smallish breasts and throat
A question mark
Kisses disorient, promise remorse
At twenty, what I don't know
About love
Would fill every lit window
From here to the river,
Winters in my maroon cape
With the little black velvet collar
In snow
Summers in a wrap-around gauze dress
Turquoise and yellow
My hair up
In a gold torque
I have read about
The hero Gilgamesh
In a narrow book
I can carry in a back pocket:
Wild man Enkidu
Who the king wants

So a harlot goes tinkling
Across the river
After that— the animals won't speak to him
Evade his touch
He's left too much
Fur, scale, feather, incisor
For the goddess of love
Her three-tiered purple skirt
Up around her waist
Inanna, Astarte, whatever
She's calling herself these days
With her cool forehead
Her nasty habit of saying good-bye
Up on the roof.

THE ART OF LOVE

3. Dido and Aeneas

He wants Rome, and she wants love
Soon, they're fucking in a cave
He sets sail, and she wants death
The land wind has an ashy breath.

THE ART OF LOVE

4. Beneath the Tracks

We still make love.
He lives
In an abandoned flat beneath the El.
He squats, he pays no rent
Has Indian rugs and copper-bottomed pans.
When he left me
I lay for three days in the mahogany four-poster bed
And wished I was dead,
Then experienced for a quarter of an hour
The purest euphoria.
First, we drink vodka
Shots from a glass
Biting a half lemon each.
He says: Miriam
Did you ever knock a wine glass off a table
And for a second think you can catch it
Until it breaks at your feet?
I say nothing.
I don't care if he lives or dies.
No, that's not true.
I wish he were dead.
We make love on the floor
Because there is no furniture
I'm on top. I keep

My earrings on, and my socks
If I had a knife
I'd carve my initials
In the floorboards.
I climb off him, and go home
My mouth tastes of lemon,
My thighs smell of sperm,
I don't care if I live or die,
Actually, I would rather live.

THE ART OF LOVE

5. *Judith and Holophernes*

He's drunk on wine, and drunk on sex
She holds the knife, knows how to kill
Baroque in red and golden lamplight
Her trust is in the god of will.

It's winter, and a town besieged
Town of virgins, virtuous,
She eats the bread and salty cheese,
Does what she must.

The Art of Love

6. Marriage

I love the crickets, the daddy longlegs
Wolf spiders, the yellow moths
That come in the cracks of the adobe
Open window, along with praying mantis
Box elder beetles, and try to live
In the shrinking summer of the house.
I know I love them because I don't kill them
Don't take a broom to corners
Or smash them with my shoe
I leave them alone.

Do I neglect you?
Young pretty women tell me I do.
But you are like old cat
Who will never run away
A sweet pea vine
That blooms faithfully
A blue Toyota that always runs
A Supremes song on the AM radio
A novel of the prairie I can read over and over.
Perhaps I do not treat you
With enough gratitude
Or follow the advice of the famous Buddhist teacher
To wake each morning

Grateful that I do not have a toothache.
I do not wake each morning and say: Thank you
I'm not single and living in San Francisco
With all my mean useless short lovers
Born under the sign of Libra.
I neglect you the way I neglect stucco
Creak in the gate, crack in my feet,
My plans to go to Peru,
These comforting things
Need little attention.

I would rather neglect you—
Otherwise you are a problem
Like a Supreme Court judge nomination
Or gallstones, or money,
Like nuclear war, or my mother.
Shouldn't a husband be more like green peas
Sunshine, an Anasazi ruin
Or the No Appointment Haircut place
Something which is perfect
That can be taken for granted.

THE ART OF LOVE

7. Danae and the Shower of Gold

He is money, golden coin
Raining down to be her man
Excessive god she cannot spend
The unstitched wound she cannot mend.

The Art of Love

8. Electra

Courtyard you can see through
To door-shaped blue of sky
White-washed walls.
History is a disaster for most of us—
Men on horseback
Against a mud village,
Fence of thorns.
My father in the Greek rooms at the museum
Was not Zeus
Had no convincing beard
Could not hurl thunder
Had to shave each morning
And splash on witch hazel.
On Sunday we looked at naked gods
He, a man so modest, he fled
If his children saw him in his pajamas.
"What do you like best
In this room?" he'd say.
It felt like a test.
Should I pick the tiny bronze
Statue of Athena with an owl
Who bursts out of her father's head
And had no mother at all?
I'm eight years old

My father loves Ancient Greece
So much that I must love
Ancient Greece
When what I really want is
Dinosaurs
Bones, those skeletons
Bigger than our house in New Jersey.
Dinosaurs, like the goddess Athena,
Have no mother, and no father
They come from eggs
They wander about
No one tells them what to do.
My father and I
Both love what is gone
He lets me buy
Whatever I want
For under five dollars in the gift shop
But I can't shake
The feeling I've failed him as a daughter.

The Art of Love

9. Europa

Girl tumbled seaward on the bull's back
Asia Minor into foam-washed Crete
She will never rest content
Until she is a continent.

THE ART OF LOVE

10. Men

Before things changed, when you
If not exactly young
Were feline, with a pair of eyebrows
Other men might kill for
Sinewy, and silver-waisted
Theseus in a maze
Wanting whatever has the head of a bull
Body of a man
Calling yourself faggot
In the old apartment
Enclosed courtyard of palms and lianas
Then, you never cruised love
Love came to you
Even the Filipino Pacific Gas and Electric man
Who came to repair the stove
Pictures of his wife and child
In the wallet in his back pocket
Could not resist you
Fell back on the linoleum
Crying like a cat.
Now, when everyone else is dead
You remember what your father said:
I was like that, too
But I didn't let it get to me

I settled down and got married.
In the snapshot he emerges from the sea
Naked torso dripping Pacific,
Cut off from other inheritance
You simply kiss
Where he would not.
And now, in a better neighborhood
You lover doesn't share your bed
His fever breaks
He's from an island
And he's going back
Across black water.
This city
Has never looked lovelier
Spread on its hills
Like a man crouched on all fours
Hercules embracing a lion.

THE ART OF LOVE

11. Echo and Narcissus

She loves him, he loves himself
She fades away, body betrayed
Reflection has him in its grip
Her voice is green leaves as they fade.

He spends his nights out in the bars
Dancing with himself, the boys
Now this nymph's promiscuous
Call, and she will answer us.

The Art of Love

12. The Sailor

Jason and the argonauts in full-blown color
Poised in snapshot
Lifting the golden fleece
Or leaning like low-riders
On old Chevys, pink fuzzy dice
Over the dash. The utter stupidity
Of heroes—
Their boats with two Egyptian eyes
Painted on the prow
Have more sense than they do
To go with the wind
Every man looks at his fate and starts running
Away from it, back into its arms
Jason loves Medea
The little hairs on his brawny arm
Don't stand up in terror at her name
He isn't halfway through
She's just a girl
She likes him
She'll do anything for love.

Once, long ago, there were two lovers
Also a golden fish and a Moslem moon
Magician in a trance

Can speak to the dead husband
Who has married again in the land of the dead
And is building a new house there.
Personally, I wish you liked me better
And didn't care so much
About getting your own way.

The Russian poet in prison
Knows her husband will wait
Out her sentence alone in the apartment
In solitary she reads her poem along the empty pipe
To common criminals, hookers and burglars
In their separate cells
And the tap tap comes back with a question
"Who is this guy Ulysses?"
That is what I want to know myself
Which one of us is on an island
With Calypso, that low-tide lady
Which one of us keeps house
In the expensive palace eternally in need of repair.
Who sails from the past, blasted like an ancient column
Who waits, who waits
Who weaves the imperfect picture
Of a dissolving re-union.

PEAK COMPLETELY
OBSCURED BY CLOUD

A line of deer at dusk
White flash under the tail
Melted patches of snow
Crossing again
Northern New Mexico
Into southern Colorado
To the east those impossible dazzling mountains
Why superimposed in the mind's eye
Skyline of New York City
Against the Rockies
Cocktail blue at 4:45 pm, some Tuesday in winter
Without rain, crossing the bridge
Suspension. Spider web. Glacier. River.

Before you can speak there is the body
A body of words:
"Duck," "kitty," "apple," "blanket."
Like the scarred underside of the yellow kitchen table
A view of feet.
For twenty years I was a slave to the alphabet
Did everything she asked me
I even believed
She was not arbitrary:
ABC.
When the stars come out under your nails

A message is waiting, deficiency
A letter has arrived, postage due
Postcard of a Greek marble stele
Tombstone of a girl who died young
Carved with a pet dove
Here it is ravens who arrange themselves on snow
Cold stars regardless of constellation
Our notion of the order of starry beasts
Starred hunters who track them.

Peak covered in snow, standing out clear
"Powdered sugar" she says
In her broken English
An edge, an alp.
Sitting in sand as if in water
Abandoned works
Of the gold mine
Baby scrabbling by prickly pear
Tiny hand, missed thorn
A dream that the child can walk,
A dream of pursuit.
Her kidney and liver
Suffer still from the abortifacts
Her mother took,
Eighth of ten children
In that crowded apartment.

Speaking of other places,
Tahiti, she says
The dream of all French schoolgirls
Who write in blue ink
Or a Tibetan village in north India
Where the woodcutters smile and wave
Cut only two boards a day
Banner of Padmasambhava
Flown red and gold on the breeze
Only once a century
Buddhism came to these people
By a mountain pass, by a trade route
Farewell to the old gods with their blue faces
108 ivory beads
Carved in the shape of human skulls so small
They might be mice or birds
The knife is vegetarian
The soup is nourishing
I'm longing for the diner in Tres Piedras
With its periwinkle blue
Pressed glass depression ware
And its kind lady behind the counter
Pouring white milk into a white glass.

THE LONESOME DEATH OF FEDERICO GARCÍA LORCA

I sweep the floorboards clean
Off Agua Fria onto Don Juan street
I took a wrong turn
Found myself lost in a tinkling neighborhood
Trees hung with a witchery
Of chimes, tin cans, bird feeders, windmills
Clamor in the mild but wintry air
Small dark knot of men
Clotted ominous on the corner
I was the intruder
Walked fast out of the hush of cigarette smoke
Past a barbed wire fence
Bright with laundry
Fuchsia shirt, sky blue pants, red vest
Splotched like Jackson Pollock
Across dry earth, blue sky.

At the age of thirty-five I dedicated myself to art
Put the baby in the stroller and went to the bodega
To buy myself one more ambiguously cool
Bottle of orange pop
To drink the sour bubbles down
On the way home
Past someone's small blue gate
Set into the adobe fence

Pale and peeling blue, or almost white
Entrancing somehow. like the inside of a mosque
A whorl, a wheel, a few
Calligraphic flowers.

Allah be with you,
They still say that
In the north hill towns
Full of dogs and dust
A place of hidden Jews
Lost Arabic. Federico García Lorca
The trouble with being dead—
A lack of tobacco and newspapers
A lack of coffee and strangers
Some sadness inside
Kept you from talking about love directly
The dead have no future but dirt
No assumption of going anywhere.

Federico García Lorca
I took your three names into my body
As a child touches snow and then her belly
Trying to eat the world
I bought your book at 179th street
And Broadway bookstore at the George
                          Washington Bridge
Bus station, Port Authority

With its frightening bathroom
Its frightening sense of frozen motion
I tried to understand your words:
Don't be named Federico
Don't go out for cigarettes
Don't get shot by fascist soldiers
Don't lie about whose mouth you want to kiss.

It's snowing
I drink the foam on the caffe latte
The Berlin wall is down
A core of the salt mine
Shows crystallized tears
From ocean 250 millions years gone
My mother wouldn't buy Spanish olives
After Franco
Everything is different now, everything is the same
The whole world says Adiós
The whole world speaks Spanish
You haven't been dead very long
But already without a shadow
You've forgotten what you can't remember
No memory of water, nor of wine.

SHELL IN THE DESERT
Rebecca Salsbury James, 1891~1968

To paint on glass
Female calla lily, rosebud
Live in the mirror's reversal
As if Taos Mountain
Were reflected in the sky
Inverted cone among stars
A woman collects nudes
Painted by men
The melancholy Russian
Paints her with a slash of lipstick
Something is bothering me
Right here, behind my heart
  "A walking woman, a waiting woman
   A mourning woman, a devout woman
   Adobe, cedar posts, old dry wood."
Cadence of earth and water
Milkweed pod on blue
Everything needs a point of reference
Her hands too crippled
For the tiny colcha embroidery stitches
How did the white conch shell
Come to rest beneath the mesa
Figure in black
Follows the narrow path
Lonely house beneath
Dark mountains, home.

Skunk Cabbage

I'd rather piss in the ocean
Than read one more word about Georgia O'Keeffe
Awaken now in a flat
In a half run-down Boston neighborhood
Put on a jade green dress
Gaudy with polka dots
Walk out in the flowering heat
In a little black lace-up shoes
Sniff the air for lilac, dogwood
And like my grandmother
Think about a small brimmed straw hat
Or a Renoir painting of an overblown
Pitcher of flowers, the pitcher
More flamboyant than cream.
All those houses we pass
Cruising at night,
Lit windows behind lace
A kind of loneliness
I haven't truly felt in years
Like Trinity Church in the rain
Across from the Public Library
A fantasy of Byzantine
Gold domes and arches, stained
Glass windows of
Five Wise Virgins
An angel distubing the pool.

Now that I am a thirty-six-year-old woman
With a husband and child
I go to the house on the island
Mayapples
With their huge glistening leaves
Under rain
Luminous in the dark
As the storm comes in
By the front porch steps
Puddle of mourning doves
In the rutted road.
Also at the museum
Two squash blossoms hung on empty space
O'Keeffe, what's there between the legs
I'm on my back
Going: do it, do it to me
It's you I love
Whistler study of young woman in gray and peach
Turn away. Georgia O'Keeffe
Could remember every color
That ever happened to her
Photographed nude
The betrayed wife, faithless husband.
Cecilia Beaux, in 1873, Philadelphia
Drew a female pelvis
For anatomy class
Paleontological skulls of camel and ass

Somehow Biblical
Drew all parts of a human skull
"How marvelous was the sphenoid
Double-winged, almost
Glittering
In its translucence
Bone seemed to be the armor
Of some creature
Whose destiny it should be to float
In a tropical ocean
Like the nautilus."
You said not to pick
Fiddlehead ferns by the stream
They were too lovely, not too many
Skunk cabbage in its own exuberance
Lights up the woods like phosphorescence
Or a landward wave. I take your hand
We're not going to die
This afternoon or even tomorrow
Two ospreys
Bring sticks to nest on the neighbor's pole
White mewing in the air
Fish for herring
Full moon insomnia
A soft warm day
White hawthorn flowers everywhere
Where land meets bay

ENCOUNTER

In the British Museum glass case
Erotic Japanese print
She is naked in the bath
Thrusts her bottom out
He slides inside her, starts to bite
Meanwhile, breathing at my elbow
Short Japanese gentleman in glasses
Stares not at her glowing buttocks
But at me, short black skirt
Wild print stockings from New York
Embarrassed, almost forty, married,
I turn to look at fans with lilies
But when he moves away
I don't go back
To motionless hot copulation in the case.

Battle for the Body
of the Daughter

Canopic jars
Divide the body up
Tomb. Vessel. Under Sirius, red dog star.
Stone calendars search for doomsday in the sky.
Worshipped as a jar.
      liver
      lungs
      intestines
      stomach
A siren is a bird with the head of a woman.
You have to start somewhere
Start with the small goddess Tonit
Just a triangle (female)
With extended arms.
Urns containing the ashes of thousands of infants.
Death pit of Ur
Full of musicians and their silver
Instruments
Ram caught in a thicket.
History changes things
Puts in a museum
Roman sarcophagus
Used locally as a water trough
Carved in peacocks
Story of Jonah

These resurrections
Of entire ships buried inland.

Iphegenia is a king's daughter
He kills her
This is just a story
Don't pay attention, or pay attention
He kills her so that the wind will change
The wind has been blowing and blowing
In a bad direction
Down east, sirocco, Santa Ana, chinook
Bad direction for his warriors' destination.

These pedestals stink of war.
Marble pediment or not
Centaur treading down a Lapith
Parthenon. Metope.
It may be glorious
But static
As the figure called cycladic
Marble mummy without features speech or motion
What am I afraid of?

Gestational memory—
Primal scene in the hallway
By the closed bedroom door
Where I sleepwalk

Five-year-old child
I want my mother and my father has her
This is no place to tell lies
Elgin marble where the nude is draped
Sad horses of the moon
Sink down
Generation born to war,
After the funeral of a contemporary.

With breasts no mother can approve of
She mourns
In black
Called whore for her fishnets
The dress with red cherries
Buttons covered in fabric
I loved...
In the far distance a temple
With four Ionic columns
Three female figures
Poised to represent the winds
That won't do what
Anyone wants them to do
That don't stop blowing.

THE MATISSE NETWORK

This was a dream
Huge canvas on one wall
Morocco, Moorish archway
Lines of black and purple
In the dream the child says:
I don't understand it
In the dream the zen master says:
I will explain it
This boundary, lintel, border-line
It is the Matisse network
Every line and color
Corresponds to something
In the waking world
Purple moon is really
Tractor trailers warming up
Outside the window
Red square is a flock of sparrows
Under your adobe eaves
Liminal as dusk, purple as asters
I will explain it
Dream just a map of morning
You wake into:
For this yellow window is the smell of coffee.

BELSHAZZAR'S FEAST

Years ago
I saw this painting with you
In London
After you had sailed a yacht
To Ireland across north Atlantic
Kept a diary for me to read
An interrupted sleep full of whales
I loved you
I wanted to be
Anywhere with you
Sleeping on the edge of misty fields
Eating vegetable soup in pubs.
They're drunk, you said,
The people in this painting are drunk
And you were right
I see it now
Rembrandt's Belshazzar
King of Babylon
Wine spills from the Temple in Jerusalem
Behind the king's shoulder
God's literate hand writes
Luminous letters from right to left
Mene Mene Tekel Upharsin
You have weighed in the balance.

The people in this painting are drunk
I see now how you knew
Your own father and mother
Locked you out
Of the empty expensive house
In Connecticut
So many dinnertimes
Forgot to cook
And you would not let your little sister
Accept the invitation to eat
At the neighbor's
You made her wait.

When I was a child
Each Christmastime we'd go
To the Play of Daniel
In the church on the park
Sit still in candlelight, and
Wait, watch, for the Assyrians to march
Down the aisle
Spears and helmets gleaming red
Who overthrow Belshazzar
But there is always another king
To trouble the prophet
Until the pale and stolid angel
Appears to save Daniel
Closes the lions' mouths

Their claws retract like pussycats'
Just at the end, in red and gold
Another angel appears to announce the birth of Christ
We were Jewish, and did not
Believe that part
But always went around the corner
To the cafe in the snow
For hot chocolate
And I had to pick
Only one pastry
Napoleon or chocolate eclair
Out of the shining case.

Hannibal Crossing the Alps

I sit in the red armchair
With the scratchy wool slipcover
Outside: snow, dusk, 1963 or '64
Waiting for dinner, I turn
The pages of the big art book
Propped in my small lap
Open to Turner's "Snow Storm.
Hannibal and his Army Crossing the Alps."
Even as a child, I can see
Something is terribly wrong
When elephants climb alps
Where they do not belong
Implied in snow and mist
Tumultuous shapes, crevices, the loneliness
Of fighting Rome. Next picture
Hero says good-bye to Leander
I know he is her lover
Not boyfriend, or husband
She's naked, out of bed, holding up a lantern
By the time Mr. Turner started painting
Leander was completely lost in waves and dark
Sea nymphs, foggy girls, the loss
That's why I like these shadows, vortexes
Stories of separation, white and gray distances
Losing light
I was lonely too, as anyone
In the hour before suburban night.

VILLANELLE

Junkies on Baca Street sit in the shade
Only cross the street to score
Purple iris blossoms unafraid

Vein is what a needle can't evade
Shadow by definition is obscure
Junkies on Baca Street sit in the shade

Blue chicory beside a broken spade
The steps are crumbling by the door
Purple iris blossoms unafraid

No women here, although the bed's unmade
Purple-hearted plate is from the war
Junkies on Baca Street sit in the shade

Rice and beans have been delayed
The pan is burnt, the arm is sore
Purple iris blossoms unafraid

Death, I've called collect, you gave
Poverty, what life gives more?
Junkies on Baca Street sit in the shade
Purple iris blossoms unafraid.

PASSOVER

Jews must be everywhere
Even in La Puebla, New Mexico
Where we pass Good Friday pilgrims
Wearing walkmans
Dusty along the highway.
It's shabbos, the two sets of candles
Adorn the tables
Set with sea shells
Seder means: the order
In which things happen
Egypt means: narrows
For plagues we dip our fingers in the wine
Hail kills your tomato plants
You quarrel
With a neighbor about a wall
A friend is unexpectedly in jail
Baby cries in the emergency room
Homeless men sleep in the arroyo
Stumble across Paseo to the liquor store
So drink four cups of wine
It's only the second time this year
Jews must get drunk
And lie down with our shoes off
On comfortable couches
The children are playing in the dusk
My daughter feeds a large white horse

A bunch of golden apples
Desert smells like the sea
Of sand and wind and something else
Clean and scoured
Miriam's Well
Springs within
Green oasis that must
Reappear within our hearts
Voices singing slightly off-key
This source of water
Follows us
Despite our exile, wandering.

Narrow Bridge

Rabbi Nachman says: the world
Is a narrow bridge
The worst thing — to be afraid
Diver poised on the high board
Handstand in a dark wind
Below, not just blue pool
But the face of the Rumanian
Or Chinese coach, the vision
Of the narrow street, red facade,
Noodle or pastry shop, old men
Clicking dominoes, some smoky
Far-away notion of home.
So jump, or fall
From high wire into sleep
You lie in the low bed
Rio Grande does not cease
Cutting gorge through bedrock
A narrow bridge
Two-lane, across sheer air, undivided
The sculptor says: he would
Rather be dead than alive
As if death were a beach
To sit on by the hour
Cape Cod of childhood
Or just above Big Sur
Pacific, Atlantic, Gulf of Mexico

Yes, that's where I want to go
Even if I don't know
What I'm talking about
No one knows
No one
The worst thing — for a Jew —
Is to despair
Wingspan of crow, or raven,
Beat the current of unbroken air
It's live or die, the same
Tide, high or low
The world's a narrow bridge
Of what we know.

WAILING WALL

Why, somewhere between sleep and waking
I saw myself at the wall in Jerusalem
Twenty years ago — too young and stupid
To pray, or stuff a crumpled desire
Penciled on paper into a crevice
Ululations of dark women throwing hard candy
At a bar-mitzvah. I was a stranger.
Where did I come from?
Bad tribesmen without horses,
Who cut off their foreskins
Poured blood on a stone;
Silent women with jars on their heads
Who sat at the gate
To judge and prophesy.
The jews before they knew
They were Jews
Before God spoke
When they raided cattle
Someplace unchanging and olive-colored
With far-off mountains.
The Arch of Tiberius
With its soldiers and captured menorah
Says we passed into history
And then passed out of it completely again.
Now I am sure there is a sweeper
Besides the desert wind

To clear those prayers each night
Scattered beneath the luminous Dome of the Rock
And the silver mosque
More beautiful than a woman's throat
Under the Moslem moon
And a zodiac of golden fish.
Who sweeps?
An old bent man with a broom
In a frayed black coat
He is a Charlie Chaplin
A butcher from Brooklyn
An Auschwitz survivor
A seller of falafel
He is alone but his eyes don't blink back tears
As he pushes away the prayers
Of the childless, the sick, the dispossessed
That cover the wall
With reproach, like a child's cry, a dove of hope.

Personification is Just the City You Were Born In

Death wears an overcoat
Avenue B
Pockets full of mothballs
Death wears a New York City coat
Black wool
Goes with everything
Always appropriate
Death wears gloves with the fingers cut off
Death wears a silk dress from the '30s
Death wears falsies
Death is a drag queen doing Judy Garland
                              in a black tuxedo and heels
Death smells like Chanel #5
Death smells like amyl nitrate
Death smells like gardenias
Or the lobby of a Brooklyn art deco apartment building
Death says come in
Death says: the number you have called
                              is not in working order
Death refuses to accept
Your collect call
Death eats diet pills and sushi
Death is a waiter
Death is a piece cutter
Death plays the violin

Death is panhandler
Death works for UPS
Death works for the CIA
Death loves initials
Death monograms things for mail order catalogues
Death comes to America
To find a better way to make a living
Death dreams about Shakespeare
A play in the park
Picnic on a blanket
A comedy, probably
Twelfth Night, or Measure For Measure,
Drinking a moderate chianti
Holding hands between the acts
Death dreams about a nice quiet place in the Catskills
Nothing fancy, five acres,
A big vegetable garden
A screened porch
All the grandkids come to visit
They eat outside on a redwood table
In the fading summer day.

Untitled

Not just the blue flamenco of desire or
                    the red flamenco of consummation
But the black flamenco of premonition,
                    alone in the house, late at night
It is not the green desperate flamenco of satin
Or the velvet flamenco of his eyes in sex
Not just the bars and streets of rain
With something unmistakable blinking in the neon
It's not just the gray flamenco of despair
Man praying in the arroyo or the drunk
                    asleep in the station
It's not just that the train
Is two days late, and the station master
Dreaming of the sea
3,000 miles of castanets and ululation
But that the blue flamenco of the sea
Of this lonely room implies something
Unremarkable, distant, a repetition
Eyes of the sea, and eyes of the high heeled shoes
Beat staccato
Flamenco without memory, or despair, or hope
The glass before you

Hotel Flora

I want to go to Mexico City and be mysterious and sad
I want a one-way ticket and a blank notebook
I want to stay at the Flora Hotel
Cheap, but very clean,
Hotel with an interior courtyard
Poinsettias that are taller than I am
I want to go to Mexico City and be mysterious and sad
Men, and women too, will look at me and ask
Who is that beautiful mysterious woman
And why is she sad?
Every day at five o'clock
I will walk through the Alameda Gardens
Give one American quarter to each
                    of the first three beggars
Watch the man swallow fire
I will go to the lobby with the Diego Rivera mural
Death walking on a Sunday with Mrs. Death
I will order two shots of tequila
I will drink only one
I will lick the back of my hand
Sprinkle salt on it
Lick that off
Like a child who has stayed all day at the beach
I will drink a shot of tequila with a ghost
I want to go to Mexico City with a borrowed suitcase
All my bras will be black and my underpants white

I will wash them by hand in the little sink
Hang them on the balcony to dry slowly
Smelling of diesel fumes
I will build a shrine on my bureau top;
Red plastic comb, two pesos,
Postcard of Frida Kahlo
Sequined Virgin of Guadalupe
Piece of lava, and a key
To a room that is not mine.

Issan Dorsey, I'll Say It Again

Issan Dorsey, I'll say it again,
Your name. Issan. Issan.
You were a man with three jobs:
The navy, drag queen, zen priest
In three robes sewed with golden thread
Head shaved
When you were alive
We thought of you at El Farol, or the old bar at Ernie's
Eating hot expensive tapas
Drinking whiskey, smiling
That unmistakable wicked smile
Of a saint or baby
Knockdown drag out handsome.
I told a friend of ours
After you were dead
And I'd written you a dozen letters
No mailbox could deliver
That I didn't understand you.
She said: That's because
You think Issan became a saint
After he died
But he was always a saint.
We remember you
When we think we've forgotten
My husband recklessly

Giving away spare change
To anyone who asks in the City
To his sister's chagrin —
She, a real New Yorker, insists
Each person should choose
Their homeless
The man in the cardboard box
She brings half a ham and cheese sandwich to
Each afternoon.
You were wilder than that
It took you all day
To go out for a pack of cigarettes
Stand on the corner of Castro and Market
Chatting with every street person
Enquiring after every madwoman
Who changed her underwear
On the traffic island
After you died
Your ashes were stolen,
When Angel walked into the kitchen
Wearing your poncho
I started to cry
When she gave the tiny bear
That had belonged to you
To my daughter
I cried again

Months later my three year old child
Said: Mommy, what's the name
Of your friend who is dead?
How did she remember
Issan Dorsey, I'll say it again.

BETTE DAVIS: IN OUT OF THE RAIN

Bette Davis movies, in out of the rain
All those rainy Wednesday matinees
Double features at the Castro Street Theater
I'd fold up my green paper umbrella
Come in under the gilt, art deco arc
Out of my life, my tears in cups of tea
Lovers on the peninsula, or on the beach
Sticky sand and tar on my feet
My heart broken
Everything broke my heart —
Fuchsia garden in Golden Gate Park
Even the Chinese pharmacy with its antlers and potions.

Meanwhile, Bette Davis on the screen
In a hat, veiled, black and white
In the wrong dress everyone says is red
Ending up with diphtheria, a brain tumor
Some warning that to be a woman
Who gets her own way once or twice
Is to then start suffering for life
Still, these movies cheered me up
The sherry, staircase, shipboard, Bette Davis
This was a long time ago
Before death hit that neighborhood
Before I turned to go
Straight on into a wilder life than
Solitude, those rainy Wednesday afternoons.

Frisco Blues

Pastel, luminous, nostalgic
Dream of a cathedral
City beneath the domination
Of spires, and sky
Cool mist of the sea
Rolled red through eucalyptus leaves
Good vegetable soup
Excellent coffee
Unbroken bread
Of a place called Frisco
Only in songs about whales
What am I doing
Here again
Houseguest to an old lover
I who am now a wife and mother
Of another neighborhood
Than Haight Street
Which draws a line still
Across what I will and will not
Do, green panhandle,
Tai Chi and swordswoman
In the near dark
Dawn or dusk
Plane trees by the museum
A gray kitten, and a white one
At the Japanese tea garden

Where early, before the crowds
My little girl throws pennies to the stream
Child in scarlet leggings
Throwing rice crackers
To pigeons and grackles
Climbs up to ride
First one — she calls the man
And then the other — lady
Of the pair of sphinxes
Egyptian revival, who ask
The traditional
Question:
What goes on four legs in the morning?
Dog on a leash
Legless carp, golden in the scum.

A bucketful of sunflowers
Rising by the curb
The child holds my hand in Chinatown
As does the old blind poet
We sit and eat
Steamed mushrooms on white rice
Drink hot brewed tea
Jasmine of paradise
An early lunch
As the fog lifts
And fat ladies

Speak Russian on the bus
Kuan-yin carved in jade
Or plastic
Luck that is good till it runs out
You were my luck
City that brought me love
My lucky money in the red envelope;
A city in which I can't
Imagine solitude
No small white flat
Poised on the edge
Of afternoon imagination
With a vase of anemones
Instead old lovers
With tears in their eyes
Drinking steamed milk on strong coffee
Some wave of feeling
That breaks on shore.

At times like this
Think of your own death
Or the death of a child
Try panic on for size
Try to remember
Exactly wht you saw
In the gilded face of the Buddha
Or in the heavy iron pot

Japantown cauldron
Noodles and broth
Or why the sight of the Chinese concierge
Middle-aged, her thoughts elsewhere
But carrying a bucket of dirty water
Dumping it each morning
With morning ceremony
On the small green tree
In its bricked-in square of earth
Why this particular gesture
Reminded you that you had a mother and father
And moved you, at the bus stop
Helplessly to tears.

I'll say I did not come this far west
To indulge in my regrets
My past is dead
As surely as my grandfather's was
When he moved from Summit, New Jersey
With his millions
Left the aunts and undershirted husbands
Playing cards in the yellow light of the kitchen
The Jersey night thick with tomatoes and corn
Cucumbers and kohlrabi plants
And how he never once looked back.

Who is the second person
Who is this "you"
Beloved, other, same but separate
Purse your lips into an O
Blow bubbles or a kiss
Work your way through grief's vowels
Entire alphabet
The sea is change without a margin
Even the shore
Our notion of repose
Goes on in love and solitude
Child in my mother arms
At twenty I said: I'll get what I want
At forty: I've gotten it, now what?
I could sit around all afternoon
And listen to stories of love
Sit here with you.

Margaret Sanger

1. By the River

Cambridge — a violet, an indeterminate,
A lilac sort of light at dusk
That turns the stones of bridges
Impressionist, bruised
I'm walking alone
Through streets that might have been
Wet with a half hour's rain
Just this afternoon
In the lecture hall
I started crying into my notes
Ostensibly because Margaret Sanger
Had gone to jail but really
Because when the lecturer
In Women's History
Started talking about Margaret's lovers
I started weeping over mine
Loneliness seemed so possible
A terrible
Solitude of a woman driven by fire
Burning like a torched meteor
Across time, but alone
Always alone, without the one
You can rely on
The way a child willingly

Takes the mother's hand
To cross the traffic of the square

I'm walking alone
Thinking incessantly
About the man in the white fedora
The one I love
With what I call love
A mix of lust and pain
His long dark body with ten
Long dark toes
And a tatoo of Pegasus
Winged horse who seems to rise
Eternally into the sky
Off the muscle
Of his forearm
I saw him not an hour ago
Pitching pennies
Against a stoop
Of the city's asphalt
What I want
I can't possess
Tonight, tomorrow night
It will be many years
Before I learn to want
What actually I can have
Or before his figure

Stops stepping into my dreams
To receive my nighttime longing
And my praise

Margaret Sanger —
I try to tell my friends
Over dinner
How I cried about her
I'm getting ready
To sob again
Into a plate of meat and green beans
They just laugh —
I'm the one among us
Who is supposed to know
About sex, about men,
And how to make them squeak
After us
It hit me hard
This lost day at the end of spring
The sense that you could be a heroine
And fail
Somehow that she'd loved more than one
Person terrified me
As if I knew I'd leave this river
For violet, lilac, elsewhere.

Margaret Sanger

2. My Mother's Diaphragm

My mother loved birth control, she loved it the way she loved parrot tulips or baba rum cake in a white box wrapped in red string. She felt it was just plain good, like a school milk program or a Japanese maple tree. My mother would hold her contraceptive diaphragm in her hand, where it looked like half of a sea shell or a creature that floats in a drop of sea water. This, said my mother, is a contraceptive diaphragm. And just remember that Margaret Sanger went to jail so you could have one. Who was Margaret Sanger? She was confused in my mind with the singing suffragettes of Mary Poppins, handcuffed to a wide iron fence with spikes on top. Margaret Sanger had gone to jail. My mother's eyes had that far-away look. In a minute she would be yelling about how Charlotte Bronte and Mary Wollstonecraft had died in childbirth. My mother wanted her daughters to go to Harvard instead of dying of septicemia. My mother was usually quite ladylike, but words like back-alley-coat-hanger abortion dripped from her lips as if she knew something. It became a joke. Mommy, where do babies come from? Just remember, Margaret Sanger went to jail for you. Mommy, can I go live with this guy in Boston? This is a contraceptive diaphragm. Margaret Sanger went to jail for you. In our house, it was Margaret Sanger who had suffered for us, and not Jesus Christ.

Margaret Sanger

3. Across State Lines

We cross state lines
Our bodies themselves are contraband cargo
Like cocaine, hashish
Like a precious ring you must swallow

We're fourteen, fifteen, sixteen years old
At our all girls school we have a fund
For an illegal abortion pool
For whoever must cross state lines

I have no license, I cannot drive
So take the long slow bus through autumn leaves
To the doctor who is neither cruel nor kind
An upstate clinic in deciduous trees

The illegal device must be mine
In a dream the bus of black and tan
Crosses what I didn't know I knew
My body itself is contraband

I do this for myself and not for you.

MARGARET SANGER

4. Margaret Sanger in New York

Maybe it is simply
That you were once a child
Locked out of the house
Standing on an upturned cardboard box
To look in at the window
At something dim — not
Your father and mother in bed
But your mother alone
Yowling like a cat beneath a ripped moon.

Not exactly afraid
But like that small boy
Who saw his mother
Spread her legs in blood
On a Spanish hill
After the house had fallen in an earthquake
Who as a man, famous, impossible
Painted horses screaming
In an air bombardment
As a light bulb swings crazily
Naked filament

Like him, you must return
To the scene of the crime

Open a storefront clinic
On the lower east side
With a sign in Yiddish and Italian
Proclaiming: Mothers!
Don't kill your babies —
There is a better way instead
Better than kitchen table not syringe
Bleeding on newspaper
While the other children
Watch agape from the doorway
And the women line up before dawn
One baby in the pram
One toddler on the arm
They already know
Why those horses are screaming.

MARGARET SANGER

5. My Grandmother's Uterus

Tipped, she couldn't
Conceive of America
Her feet went one way
Into the apple orchards of New Jersey
Her womb went the other way
Back to Russia and its groves of birches
Good at cards but bad at gossip
Other women wouldn't tell her anything
Thirty years old, no sons.

My other grandmother, mother's mother
Organizes a union for seamstresses
Afraid to marry, afraid of men, their ways
All night the Triangle Fire girls
Ignite and flame
Like shattered bits of stars
And fall directly
To the polished floorboards
Beneath her bed.

Emma Goldman
Is on Riker's Island again
Eating the hot meals
Her friends bring her in boxes

Tied with string
She's a heroine, and she knows it
She won't bear children
Or give a name to anything.

My grandmother's uterus
Tips back, chock full
Of sons
My other grandmother
Blacklisted, succumbs
To a husband who will button her galoshes
The lines are drawn
That lead to me
Father, mother
But sometimes in the dark even I can see
A burning girl beneath the bed
Who needs my hand to cool her head
Whose burning will not turn to ash
Who burns but is not
Consumed.

Margaret Sanger

6. *On Barren Ground*

Certainly here it must be snowing
It is winter, like those paperweights
Of snow over the Statue of Liberty
                   or the Empire State Building
This sea level, this place
In the heart I go to
When my sisters can't bear children
Sisters torn by abortions and miscarriage
With the longing that turns to hate
Other women with carts full of groceries
And whining children whose noses need wiping.

O little twin, o impossible
To conceive embryo
With our family name
O Rachel in the dark
Telling Jacob
Give me children
Or I will die
O hemorrhage, o oxygen
Rich blood that pours out
On sand
Or Snow White's mother
Pricking her finger

Bearing one daughter
Before she dies.

Is it only the Bad Queen
Who has no children?
Or the Russian poets
Starved out of ovulation
In the Siberian small zone
Or the woman with tubes torn for profit
Amazons with shields in the os of the womb
Or an entire generation of refugees
Up along the Cambodian border
Who will never bleed at all

It is like death
This not having children
Or like life/impossible

Margaret Sanger

7. My Daughter

She startled her father in the De Vargas mall
By saying loudly as she held his hand
That she knew where babies came from:
Peanuts, she shouted
Come out of your penis
And make a baby
With mommy's egg!
Her father, a shy man, was forced to mumble
Not peanuts
As passers-by laughed

She draws her name
Large balloons or wombs
With tiny knots on the side
Like belly buttons
Inside each enclosure
Is a letter
H, I, and L
These are the letters she can write
They spell my name, she says
H, I, L.
No. I say
Your name is I-S-A-B-E-L

She looks at me in pure disgust
I do it the *easy* way, she says.

When she looks out the window she gasps
Suddenly almost sobbing
Mommy, she says, mommy
The chimpanzees are dead
I come running
Expecting large primates strewn on the front lawn
She points to the flower planter,
A withered purple pansy
Pansy, I say, pansy
Not chimpanzee
She looks at me in disbelief

Half the time I feel I'm lying
Where do babies come from?
Why did our friend die?
Why is a lie bad?
How do you spell Isabel?
I too want to
Do it the easy way.

MARGARET SANGER

8., Margaret Sanger in Egypt

Margaret Sanger in Egypt
By the light of the pyramids and sphinx
By the pale purple light
Like panacea, salt for meat
She's blurry in the photograph
Wearing a large and billowy hat
Like someone's great aunt
At a late afternoon garden party
Margaret Sanger does not need to read
Her horoscope in the daily paper
All twelve signs of the zodiac
Imprint themselves in gold on her skirt
She is Fortune with her globe
Rising out of the Venetian bay
She is the ring the *doge*
Throws from a gondola to the sea
Once she was a bride
Who did not stand
Beneath the huppa, sacred tent
But simply went
To the justice of the peace and took a Jewish groom
Into her Irish name
Her only daughter is dead
She blames herself

The loss goes on and on
Like breath inside her body

A plate of pomegranates and eggs
Forget the god of virgin birth
Isis is the one who seeks
What's rendered among reed and rush
What clings like sediment at bottom
Of this Pandora's jar
Is Hope
Who stays among us without wings
The river is high, then ebbing low
Cambridge, or Nile
Implying lights
Of city scattered on the rim
At dusk
Whose feathered winds must
Clasp us close
A mother's touch.

Pocahontas Looks Down From The Air

I see America laid out like money
Squares of snow and grain
This plane will not crash
Too many nuns and soldiers,
Still, flying out of Denver
I sit over the wing
The way my mother told me
Because it is safer.
Down onto dry aquifer valley
Range of southern Rockies
Big snow-covered Buddha, uncontained
In trackless sky
I remember snowballs
Those tiny plastic domes
With the Statue of Liberty
Or a rainbow saying Colorado
Shake it
Glitter snow falls
Cape Cod in a bottle
Snow on fishes and mermaids
Or just go to Ben Franklin craft store
Get a tiny plastic spruce and tiny plastic deer
Epoxy them to the lid of a baby food jar
Cover it all with cotton balls
Fill jar with water and sprinkles
Turn it upside down.

The past
Is too complicated
To contain.
My father was a king
I saved the life of a man.
Both old men are dead.
And this valley
Has sucked out all the water
From its subterranean cavern.

POCAHONTAS ELECTRIC

I was my father's daughter
Frozen river, able to travel
Long cold distance
Without complaint, or hint of thaw

Woman among the men
Female with a bitter tongue
Motherless story
Of a girl who'll do anything

Talkative, constrained,
I was his arrow, his son
What I've learned may bear me out
But not help me bear down.

Pocahontas Has a Baby/Peace

I want to just stay on the island
Strawberries, oysters, grapes and clams
The size of my fist
Birth like a low tide
Birth like a freight train, a diesel truck
Ninety miles an hour after midnight
I have a baby
Vision of raccoon
Rattling cans outside in the dark
Green eyes with fire swamp fox
I am not about to trade Manhattan
For a necklace of glass
White beads and blue beads
I prefer
Rain to drought
Peace to war
Corn to a harsh word
Although the dead stingray
Is a map of the deep
And those cold high passes
Where we roast and eat our dead
On the last of the fuel
Ancestors whose bones will eat
Us whole and dry
Take the gris-gris
White wings of the ship

Marry me to the brown man of tobacco
Give me a new name — Rebecca
The woman at the well
The woman who offers water
In a gourd dipper
Mother of nations
Stranger, bride, bearing a tribe
For each sign of the zodiac
And call this marriage
Peace of Pocahontas.

Pocahontas on Baca Street

All night in bed alone
I think about parsley
Sunday morning take the baby
To Agua Fria Nursery
Fill earthen pots
With chives, mint, lavender
Dirt is not dirty
I tell my daughter,
Cut leeks and potatoes
For a soup.
Leftover snow, and a hazy moon
Today I remember
Every quarrel
Every gold and silver shell
Picked up from the island shore
How I must have wanted something.
On Baca Street
Two Greek columns stand
In front of an adobe warehouse
Holding up nothing
But a blue illusion of sky.
I miss low tide, the way it smells
Here in high desert
No low tide for aeons
Small shells in limestone
Ring of fossil mountains

The sea got out of here
A long time ago
When the getting was good
And went someplace else
To make a living.

POCAHONTAS: HER VISION OF THE BEAR

She bear in spring tide
Red gill river
Like the underside
Of mushroom, potent soma

Salmon flapping cerulean
Roe among gulls
Summer's stranded fish
For winter fat gestation

She bear who carries
Fertile egg toward hibernation
Who like the moon, lives off something
Flesh we can only imagine

Ursus in the constellation
Cubs of stars in aviation
Over the continent, who is the continent
America, the impermanent.

COLOPHON

■ ■ ■ ■ ■ ■ ■

Set in *Minion*, designed by Robert Slimbach,
the classicism of this face echoes Renaissance type families
as its technical grace imparts a pure, bright color to every word.
Titling is in *New Caledonia* Old Style small capitals,
a new adaptation of the luxuriant *Caledonia*
originally designed by W. A. Dwiggins in *1938*.
Book design by J. Bryan

Miriam Sagan lives in Santa Fe, New Mexico
with her husband Robert Winson, a zen priest,
and their daughter Isabel. Her books of poetry include
AEGEAN DOORWAY (Zephyr Press, 1984),
TRUE BODY (Parallax Press, 1991), and
BABY BABY (with Judy Katz-Levine, Noctiluca Press, 1994).